THAT'S THE JOB FOR ME!

I'M GOING TO BE A BALLET DANCER!

BY MICHOU FRANCO

Gareth Stevens PUBLISHING

Please visit our website, www.garethstevens.com. For a free color catalog of all our high-quality books, call toll free 1-800-542-2595 or fax 1-877-542-2596.

Library of Congress Cataloging-in-Publication Data

Names: Franco, Michou, author.
Title: I'm going to be a ballet dancer! / Michou Franco.
Description: Buffalo, NY : Gareth Stevens Publishing, 2025. | Series: That's the job for me! | Includes index.
Identifiers: LCCN 2023033146 (print) | LCCN 2023033147 (ebook) | ISBN 9781538293263 (library binding) | ISBN 9781538293256 (paperback) | ISBN 9781538293270 (ebook)
Subjects: LCSH: Ballet dancing–Juvenile literature. | Ballet–Vocational guidance–Juvenile literature. | Ballerinas–Juvenile literature. | Ballet–Juvenile literature.
Classification: LCC GV1787.5 .F62 2025 (print) | LCC GV1787.5 (ebook) | DDC 792.8–dc23/eng/20230721
LC record available at https://lccn.loc.gov/2023033146
LC ebook record available at https://lccn.loc.gov/2023033147

Published in 2025 by
Gareth Stevens Publishing
2544 Clinton Street
Buffalo, NY 14224

Designer: Claire Zimmermann
Editor: Therese Shea

Photo credits: Cover, pp. 1, 7 antoniodiaz/Shutterstock.com; Series Art (background) Salmanalfa/Shutterstock.com; pp. 5, 21 VGstockstudio/Shutterstock.com; p. 9 PeopleImages.com - Yuri A/Shutterstock.com; p. 11 Charly Morlock/Shutterstock.com; p. 13 vgajic/iStock; p. 15 Igor Bulgarin/Shutterstock.com; p. 17 wundervisuals/iStock; p. 19 df028/Shutterstock.com.

Printed in the United States of America

CPSIA compliance information: Batch #CS25GS: For further information contact Gareth Stevens, New York, New York at 1-800-542-2595.

CONTENTS

Boldface words appear in the glossary.

Becoming a Ballet Dancer

I love to dance, and I love to **perform**. I love music, and I love to wear **costumes**. And I really love **ballet**. So, I'm going to be a ballet dancer. Let me tell you how I'll do it!

School First

I'll start out taking a class at a dance school. I'll learn ballet technique, or basic movements and skills. As I become more skilled, I'll enter dance **competitions**. Some winners get **scholarships** to famous ballet academies, or schools!

Ballet academies prepare young dancers to become **professional** dancers. Some ask students to audition before they can join the academy. An audition is like a test. But instead of writing, dancers perform. They're judged on their skills. If they're skilled enough, they can attend the academy.

Join the Company

Ballet academies train students even more. The older the student, the more classes they take. After a time, they audition to join a ballet company. A company is a group of dancers that stages, or puts on, ballets. Anyone can audition to join a company.

Rehearsals

Companies pay dancers to perform. Dancers may have six to nine hours of **rehearsal** each day. That's a lot of practice! They may learn parts for many ballets at first. Then, they **focus** on the ballet they will perform next.

Performances

When it's time to perform the ballet, the dancers still practice most days. On a performance day, they begin with about three hours of rehearsal. After a ballet's performances are done, dancers may get a week off. Then, rehearsals begin for the next ballet.

Time Off

A ballet company often does a number of ballets a year. Then, the dancers have some more time off. Some dance with another company. Some teach ballet. Others like to get a job that is completely different! They let their body rest.

Principals

Most dancers in the company start out in the dance corps (KOHR). They dance as a group. As a dancer gets better, they may perform **solos**. The best dancers in a company become principals. They get the leading parts in a ballet.

I Can Do It!

It might take me 10 years to join a ballet company. Until then, I'll keep practicing. I'll get stronger. I'll build **stamina**. I'll enter competitions. I'll do what I can to become a better dancer. See you on the stage!

GLOSSARY

ballet: A kind of dancing performed on a stage that often uses dance and music to tell a story.

competition: An event in which people try to win.

costume: Clothes for a performance that someone uses to look like someone else.

focus: To direct your effort to something.

perform: To play music, sing, or dance for others.

professional: Earning money from an activity that many people do for fun.

rehearsal: A practice for a later performance.

scholarship: Money awarded to a student to pay for their education.

solo: A performance by one artist.

stamina: The strength needed to do something for a long time.

FOR MORE INFORMATION

BOOKS

Allman, John Robert. *Boys Dance.* New York, NY: Doubleday Books for Young Readers, 2020.

Bouder, Ashley. *Welcome to Ballet School.* Beverly, MA: Frances Lincoln Children's Books, 2020.

WEBSITES

Ballet
kids.britannica.com/kids/article/ballet/352818
Learn more about the positions and history of ballet.

What Is Ballet?
www.pbt.org/learn-and-engage/resources-audience-members/ballet-101/what-is-ballet/
Read about the different kinds of ballet.

Publisher's note to educators and parents: Our editors have carefully reviewed these websites to ensure that they are suitable for students. Many websites change frequently, however, and we cannot guarantee that a site's future contents will continue to meet our high standards of quality and educational value. Be advised that students should be closely supervised whenever they access the internet.

INDEX